Celebrate!

Diwali

Mike Hirst

HODDER
Wayland

CHINESE NEW YEAR

CHRISTMAS

ID-UL-FITR

**All Wayland books encourage children
to read and help them improve their literacy.**

✓ The contents page, page numbers, headings and
index help locate specific pieces of information.

✓ The glossary reinforces alphabetic knowledge and
extends vocabulary.

✓ The 'finding out more' section suggests other books
dealing with the same subject.

This book is based on the original title **Diwali** in the
Festivals series, published in 1996 by Wayland Publishers Ltd.

Editor: Philippa Smith
Designers: Tim Mayer and Malcolm Walker

First published in 1999 by Wayland Publishers Ltd,
This Edition published in 2001 by Hodder Wayland,
an imprint of Hodder Children's books
© Hodder Wayland 1999
This paperback edition published in 2002

British Library Cataloguing in Publication Data
Hirst, Mike
   Diwali. – (Celebrate!)
   1. Diwali – Juvenile literature
   I. Title
   294.5'36

ISBN 0 7502 4206 X

Cover picture: During the festival of Diwali, Hindus light
little clay lamps, called diwas.

Picture acknowledgements
Cephas: M. Dutton 29 (bottom right); Circa Photo Library: 13
(bottom), 19 (top), 24 (top), 25; Hutchison Library: Liba Taylor
15 (top), McIntyre 29 (bottom left); James Davis Worldwide
Photographic Library: 5, 11; Eye Ubiquitous: David Cumming
10, Tim Hawkins 23; Life File: Andrew Ward 12, 23 (top); Bipin
J Mistry: 18 (bottom), 27; Christine Osborne: 7, 18 (top), 20
(top), 22 and title page; Ann and Bury Peerless: 16, 20 (bottom);
Trip: Dinodia *cover*, 6, 13 (top), H Rogers 8, 9, 13 (top), 14, 15
(both), 17,(bottom), 26, 29 (top), L Clarke 21 (top).
Border and cover artwork by Tim Mayer.

Contents

Words that appear in **bold** in the text
are explained in the glossary on page 30.

Diwali Around the World

The Hindu religion is very old. We think it began in the Indus Valley, in India, about 4,000 years ago. Today, it is still the biggest religion in India. Many **Hindus** have also gone to live in other parts of the world, as this map shows. They have taken their religion with them.

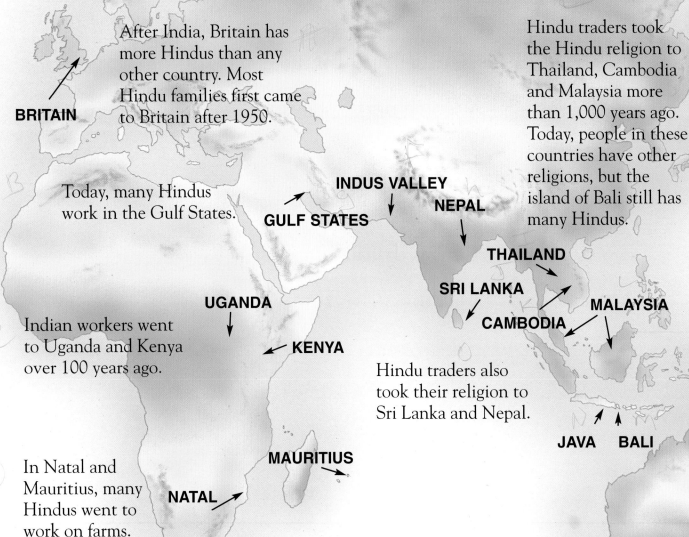

After India, Britain has more Hindus than any other country. Most Hindu families first came to Britain after 1950.

BRITAIN

Hindu traders took the Hindu religion to Thailand, Cambodia and Malaysia more than 1,000 years ago. Today, people in these countries have other religions, but the island of Bali still has many Hindus.

Today, many Hindus work in the Gulf States.

INDUS VALLEY

GULF STATES

NEPAL

THAILAND

SRI LANKA

UGANDA

CAMBODIA

MALAYSIA

Indian workers went to Uganda and Kenya over 100 years ago.

KENYA

Hindu traders also took their religion to Sri Lanka and Nepal.

JAVA **BALI**

MAURITIUS

In Natal and Mauritius, many Hindus went to work on farms.

NATAL

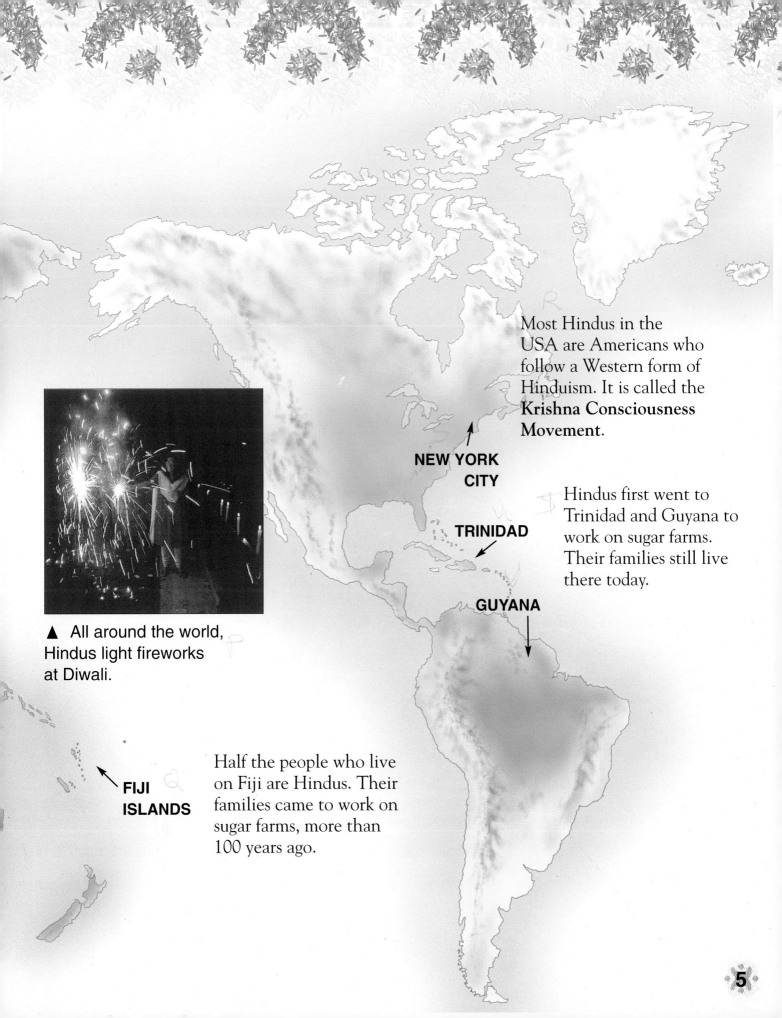

Most Hindus in the USA are Americans who follow a Western form of Hinduism. It is called the **Krishna Consciousness Movement**.

NEW YORK CITY

TRINIDAD

Hindus first went to Trinidad and Guyana to work on sugar farms. Their families still live there today.

GUYANA

▲ All around the world, Hindus light fireworks at Diwali.

FIJI ISLANDS

Half the people who live on Fiji are Hindus. Their families came to work on sugar farms, more than 100 years ago.

Welcome to Diwali

Every year, Hindus look forward to the festival of Diwali. It is a happy time in the Hindu religion.

◄ These little clay lamps are called **diwas**. Hindus light diwas at Diwali.

Diwali is sometimes called the 'Festival of Light'. It happens in October or November, when the nights are cool and dark in India. Celebrations sometimes last for five days.

▲ Many Hindu families have pictures of their favourite gods at home.

The Hindu religion has many gods. Hindus believe that all of these gods show them how to live a good life.

Different gods are worshipped in different parts of India. But for all Hindus, Diwali celebrations are similar. It is a time of hope and new beginnings.

Diwali Gods

◄ Vishnu is an important god who cares for the world. Hindus believe he came to earth ten times, in different **incarnations**. This is Vishnu when he came to earth as Prince Rama. Rama's wife, Sita, is at his side.

Some gods are especially important at Diwali. The favourite Diwali story is about how the god Vishnu came to earth as Prince Rama.

◄ Vishnu once came to earth as the god Krishna. Krishna played a flute. His beautiful music made people very happy.

Prince Rama had a wicked stepmother. She sent Rama away from his kingdom so that her own son could become king.

One day, a demon called Ravana kidnapped Rama's wife, Sita. Rama went to rescue her from the island where Ravana lived.

Rama was helped by Hanuman, the monkey god. Hanuman attacked Ravana with a big army of monkeys. At the end of the battle, Rama killed Ravana with a magic bow and arrow.

After the battle, Rama went back to his kingdom. The people saw he was a great leader and made him king.

◄ Hanuman, leader of the monkey army.

During the battle, Ravana tried to set Hanuman's tail on fire. But Hanuman just ran around Ravana's city, and set the houses on fire instead.

▲ Hindus have fireworks at Diwali. The fireworks remind them of Rama's battle against Ravana.

Candles and Lights

At Diwali, Hindus put lights around their houses and **temples**. The lights remind them of the story about Prince Rama. The lights show Rama the way home to his kingdom.

Everyone wants to welcome Rama into their home, too.

The lights tell the gods that the people in the houses are ready for them.

▼ Colourful electric lights on a temple in India.

Temple Lights

In the past, oil lamps and candles were the only lights used for Diwali. Today, many Hindu temples and homes have electric lights as well.

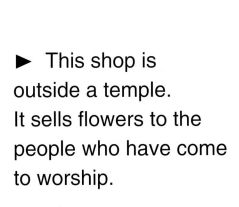

► This shop is outside a temple. It sells flowers to the people who have come to worship.

On the first day of Diwali, people light just one lamp. This light is for Yama, the god of death.

The god Yama helps Hindus to remember their friends and relatives who have died.

Traditional Diwali lamps are made out of clay or metal. They have the shape of a small dish. There is oil or butter inside the dish.

▲ This metal diwa has butter inside.

Wealth and Success

◄ Lakshmi was born in the sea. She is the wife of Vishnu. If you look carefully you can see the pictures of Vishnu's ten incarnations in this picture.

Diwali is the time of Lakshmi's birthday. Lakshmi is the goddess who brings good luck. She makes people rich and successful.

▲ Hindus often give each other Diwali cards like these.

In southern India, Lakshmi is very popular. On her birthday, women sit outside their houses with flaming torches and sing songs for her.

Lakshmi's birthday is also a busy time for business people and shopkeepers. They write down what they have bought and sold, and work out how much money they have made during the year. Then they show their account books to the goddess.

▼ Businessmen with their account books at Diwali.

Good Luck

Some people play cards at Diwali. They hope that the goddess Lakshmi will bring them good luck, so that they win.

Hindu Clothes

Many Hindus wear traditional clothes.

Women wear a long dress called a sari.
They often have lots of jewellery.

Men wear a baggy shirt called a kurta. Instead
of trousers, some men wear a cloth tied round
their waist. It is called a dhoti.

▼ Women draw patterns
on their hands. They use
a brown dye called henna.

Some people like to have new clothes for Diwali. Hindus who live in villages make special journeys into town to buy new clothes.

Bright colours are very popular. In some parts of India, people print patterns on cloth using carved wooden blocks.

In other areas, material is decorated with tiny mirrors and sequins.

▲ Buying material to make a new sari.

▶ These clothes have patterns made with silver and gold thread.

Food

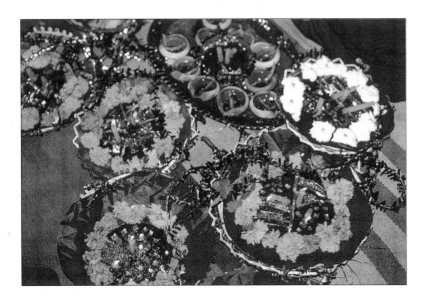

◄ A colourful Diwali meal decorated with flowers.

Food is an important part of the Diwali festival. Everybody makes special food for any visitors who come to their home.

Most Hindus do not eat meat. They respect all the different kinds of life on earth. They do not like to kill animals, so they are vegetarians.

Indian food is usually spicy. People add spices such as chillies and ginger to vegetables and lentils. A spicy Indian dish is called a curry.

▲ A thali plate holds lots of different foods.

Some families have a thali meal at Diwali. A thali is a big plate. People choose different curries to put on their thali.

◄ These girls have a mix of Western snacks, such as crisps and lollipops, and Indian snacks.

They also eat rice and a kind of round, flat bread called chappati. The favourite drink is lassi. Lassi is made out of yoghurt.

Sweets are important at Diwali. Hindus love sweets, and they take them as presents when they go to visit friends and family. Most Indian sweets are soft and sticky.

Savoury snacks are popular at Diwali, too. A small meal of tea and snacks is called tiffin.

Diwali Traditions

◄ This shop sells garlands for Diwali. A garland is a necklace of flowers.

In India, Diwali is a time for being at home with family and friends.

Before the festival, Hindus clean their homes.

Hindus also decorate the ground outside their homes with **rangoli patterns**. Rangoli patterns are made with coloured powder and paste.

Inside their homes, Hindus have small statues of their favourite gods. At Diwali, the family meets to say prayers to these gods.

▲ Making rangoli patterns.

Hindus begin each day of Diwali by washing carefully. They put on their best clothes.

Sometimes Hindus wear necklaces of flowers. They also put special oils in their hair to make it smell beautiful.

▲ In Indonesia, people tell the Diwali story with shadow puppets.

Some families go out to watch actors put on a play out of doors. The play tells the Diwali story about Prince Rama. There are fireworks at the end of the play.

Rangoli Patterns

All of these Rangoli patterns are popular at Diwali.

 Swastika For Hindus, this is a sign that means good luck.

 Om This is a holy word. Hindus often say it as part of their prayers.

 Lotus flower The lotus flower stands for Lakshmi, the goddess of wealth and good luck.

Diwali in the Temple

Sometimes Hindu friends and families live a long way from one another. But they still want to get together at Diwali, so they meet up at a temple.

When visitors get to the temple, they ring the temple bell. Each person goes up to one of the gods and says a quiet prayer. Visitors offer small plates of flowers and food to the gods.

▲ This woman visiting a temple is wearing her best sari.

Today, many Hindus live outside India. In Britain and North America, the wintry weather is too cold to have the Diwali festival out of doors. A temple is a warm place where Hindus can celebrate indoors.

◄ Visitors in a temple have left these sweets and flowers as gifts for the gods.

▲ Krishna worshippers in New York, USA.

Krishna Worship

In the USA, many Hindus are Americans who worship the god Krishna. At Diwali, the Krishna worshippers go to the Krishna temple in New York. They wear orange robes and beads.

Krishna worshippers sing a song to show their love for the gods. They sing the words 'Rama' and 'Krishna' over and over again.

Hari Krishna, Hari Krishna,
Krishna, Krishna, Hari, Hari.
Hari Rama, Rama, Rama,
Rama Rama, Hari Hari.

Diwali is also a time for dancing. Older Hindus teach the dances to children and young people.

The older people want everyone to know about their traditions. Even if young Hindus have never been to India, it is important for them to learn about their family's religion.

◄ Some Indian dances tell religious stories. These children are dressed as Hindu gods to dance out the story of Krishna.

Diwali in Trinidad

Trinidad is an island in the Caribbean. It has people from many religions: Hindus, Muslims and Christians.

At Diwali Hindus invite everyone to the festival. It takes place out of doors, where everybody can join in. Everyone puts up tall bamboo poles. The poles have diwas on top. All the buildings on the island have Diwali lights. Diwali is about good winning over evil. The people of Trinidad celebrate with a carnival of music and dancing.

▲ Children learn the dandia raas dance.

The dandia raas is a popular dance. Everyone has two sticks, called dandias. They tap the sticks together in time to the music. As the music gets faster, so does the banging of the sticks.

It is a difficult dance. It is easy to hit somebody by mistake, so you have to bang the sticks at just the right time.

Sikh Diwali

The Sikh religion comes from India. Like Hindus, **Sikhs** also have a festival at Diwali.

The holy men in the Sikh religion are called **gurus**. At Diwali, Sikhs remember the life of a guru called Harogobind Sahib.

An emperor put put Harogobind in prison because of his religion. When Harogobind was let out of jail, he asked for 52 Hindu kings to be let out with him.

▲ Harogobind Sahib was a soldier as well as a holy man. Can you see his sword?

◄ The Sikh Golden Temple at Amritsar, in India. Thousands of Sikhs come here for Diwali.

At Diwali, Sikhs go to a temple, called a **gurdwara**. The gurdwara has a big kitchen, so that everyone can eat a meal together.

Sikhs also sing religious songs, and read from their holy books. At the end of the festival, there is a big firework display.

The Hindu Calendar

There are many Hindu gods and goddesses, and there are many festivals. Some festivals are quite small, and happen in just one part of India. Other festivals are important for all Hindus. Many Hindus take part in these large festivals.

Hindus have twelve months in every year, but their calendar is different from the Christian calendar. For Hindus, the first month is in spring.

Chiatra or New Year Festival
March or April
This festival marks the start of the Hindu calendar and is meant to bring good luck.

Rama Navami (Rama's Birthday)
April or May
This festival remembers the day when Prince Rama was born.

Ratha Yatra
June or July
The god Krishna is called 'Jagannath' or 'Lord of the World'. On this day, Hindus take statues of Krishna out of the temple. They put him on a cart, or chariot, and take him on a journey around their village or town.

Rakasha Bandhan or Sisters and Brothers' Day
July or August
On this day, girls tie a thread around their brothers' wrists. They believe the threads will keep away evil. Boys give presents to their sisters.

Janmashtami or Krishna's Birthday
August or September
This festival celebrates the day that Krishna was born.

▲ Ganesh Chaturthi

August or September

On this day, Hindus worship Ganesh, a god with the head of an elephant.

Vavaratru/Dusserah/Durga Puja

September or October

A nine-day festival to worship the mother goddess. She is called Kali, Parvati, and Durga in different parts of India.

◄ At this time Hindus also remember Rama's battle with Ravana.

Mahashivratri

January or February

This festival is for the god Shiva, who makes new things and destroys old ones. Hindus believe Shiva created the world.

▼ Holi or Spring Festival

February or March

At Holi, Hindus give thanks for the crops that grow in the winter. It is a time for fun and jokes. There is a special bonfire, and people throw water and coloured powder at one another.

Glossary

diwas   Small lamps, usually made out of clay.

gurdwara   A Sikh temple – a building where Sikhs go to meet and worship together.

gurus   Religious teachers in the Hindu and Sikh religions.

Hindus   People who follow the Hindu religion and worship the Hindu gods.

incarnation   Hindus believe that when somebody dies, they are born again in a different body. Each body of that person is called an incarnation. Some gods have many bodies too.

Krishna Consciousness Movement
A group of Hindus who worship the god Krishna. Many members of the group do not live in India.

rangoli patterns   Colourful patterns that Hindus paint outside houses and temples on special occasions.

Sikhs   People who belong to the Sikh religion. Sikhs and Hindus worship in different ways, although they often have festivals on the same day.

temples   Special places with statues of gods inside. Hindus go to temples to worship the gods.

Finding Out More

BOOKS TO READ

Celebration! by Barnabas and Anabel Kindersley (Dorling Kindersley, 1997)

Celebrate Hindu Festivals by Dilip Kadodwala and Paul Gateshill (Heinemann, 1995)

Feasts and Festivals by Jacqueline Dineen (Dragons World, 1995)

A Flavour of India by Mike Hirst (Wayland, 1998)

India by Susie Dawson (Watts, 1998)

My Hindu Faith by Anita Ganeri (Evans, 1999)

My Hindu Life by Dilip Kadodwala and Sharon Chhapi (Wayland, 1996)

My Sikh Life by Manju Aggrawal (Wayland, 1996)

What Do We Know About Hinduism? by Anita Ganeri (Macdonald Young Books, 1995)

The World of Festivals by Philip Steele (Macdonald Young Books, 1996)

EXHIBITIONS OF HINDU ART

The British Museum, Great Russell Street, London WC1B 3DG   Tel: 0207 636 1555

The Victoria and Albert Museum, Cromwell Road, London SW7 2RL   Tel: 0207 938 8500

USEFUL ADDRESSES

The Commonwealth Institute, London W8 6NQ Tel: 0207 603 4535

Krishna Consciousness, Correspondence Secretary, Croome House, Sandown Road, Watford, Hertfordshire WD2 4XA

OTHER RESOURCE MATERIAL

Festivals Worksheets by Albany Bilbe and Liz George (Wayland, 1998)

Twenty-five pages of photocopiable, copyright-free worksheets on the topic of festivals, together with teachers' notes and topic web.

The SHAP Working Party on world religions can supply a calendar of religious festivals; religious artefacts and photopacks on different beliefs. The SHAP Working Party c/o The National Society's RE Centre, 36 Causton Street, London SW1P 4AU Tel: 0207 932 1194   Fax: 0207 932 1199

Religious artefacts and posters can be bought from Articles of Faith, Bury Business Centre, Kay Street, Bury BL9 6BU Tel: 0161 705 1878

Books and Hindu music can be bought from The Institute of Indian Art and Culture, The Bhavan Centre, 4a Castletown Road, West Kensington, London W14 9HQ Tel: 0207 381 3086.

The Festival Shop stocks all kinds of educational material relating to festivals. It also publishes *The Festival Year* annually, a multifaith spiral calendar of festivals. The Festival Shop, 56 Poplar Road, Kings Heath, Birmingham B14 7AG Tel: 0121 444 7AG   Fax: 0121 441 5404

Index